THE FACTS ON HALLOWEEN

John Ankerberg
& John Weldon

HARVEST HOUSE PUBLISHERS
Eugene, Oregon 97402

Cover by Terry Dugan Design, Minneapolis, Minnesota.

THE FACTS ON HALLOWEEN

Copyright © 1996 by The John Ankerberg Show
Published by Harvest House Publishers
Eugene, Oregon 97402

ISBN 1–56507–512–9

Printed in the United States of America.

96 97 98 99 00 01 02 /LP/ 10 9 8 7 6 5 4 3 2 1

CONTENTS

Preface

Preface

"Trick or Treat!" Which one of us doesn't remember the glee and adventure of dressing up in various costumes in order to canvas the neighborhood for as many goodies as we could possibly capture? The adults seemed to enjoy it as much as we did.

In a marketing sense, Halloween today has become big business. As a recent page one article in *Advertising Age* observed, "It's enough to give Santa a scare." The article revealed that the second most popular event for marketing activity, behind Christmas, is now Halloween. Halloween is currently a 2.4-billion-dollar merchandising bonanza. Fifty percent of all Americans will decorate for Halloween (80 percent do for Christmas). Besides the kids, at least one in three adults will buy costumes for themselves. And among adults, Halloween has become the third most popular party activity behind the Superbowl and New Year's Eve.[1] Not surprisingly, Halloween is also National Magic Day observed by magicians everywhere.

But today, some people are confused over the issue of Halloween. Do its pagan and occult associations disqualify it spiritually or ethically as an activity that Christians can participate in? In this booklet, we will examine the origin of Halloween, its historic and contemporary relation to paganism and the occult, its symbols, and the phenomena associated with Halloween, such as ghosts. We will also provide biblical and other guidelines for evaluating this activity.

Section I
Halloween: Ancient, Medieval, and Modern

1. What is the origin of Halloween?

In A.D. 835, Pope Gregory IV designated November 1 as All Saints Day or All Hallow's Day (the term Hallow refers to saints). The day before this, October 31, was known as All Hallow's Evening. How did we get the condensed term "Halloween"? Look at the phrase "All Hallow's Evening." If we drop the word "all," the "s" on Hallow's and the "v" and "ing" on evening, the result spells Halloween.

Long before the church gave this name to the evening before All Saints Day (a celebration in remembrance of saints and martyred saints), it had been celebrated in various ways in many places around the world. One writer is correct when she observes that it "probably combines more folk customs the world around than will ever be sorted out, catalogued and traced to their sources."[2]

It is generally agreed that, in church history, Halloween took the place of a special day celebrated by the ancient Druids, who were the learned or priestly class of the Celtic religion.* The Celts were the first Aryan people who came from Asia to settle in Europe. In fact, we can see certain similarities between Druidism and the religion of India: "Celtic religion, presided over by the Druids (the priestly order) presents beliefs in various nature deities and certain ceremonies and practices that are similar to those in Indian religion. As in Hinduism, the Druids also believed in reincarnation, specifically in the transmigration of the soul, which teaches that people may be reborn as animals."[3]

These Celtic people lived in northern France and the British Isles. They engaged in occult arts, worshiped nature, and gave it supernatural, animistic qualities. Certain trees or plants, such as oak and mistletoe, were given great spiritual significance. (According to Celtic authority Lewis Spence, the original meaning of the term druid implies a priest of the oak-cult.) Interestingly, fully ninety percent of the world's sometimes mysterious "crop circles" lie within the geographical proximity of the ancient and possibly druidic ruins of Stonehenge. At least some of these phenomena may be considered supernatural.

The Celts worshiped the Sun God (Belenus) especially on *Beltane*, May 1, and they worshiped another god, apparently

---

* Some facts about the Druids are disputed or uncertain; there are differences plus geographical peculiarities between early and late Druidism.

the Lord of Death or the Lord of the Dead, on *Samhain,* October 31. Beltane ("Fire of Bel") was the time of the Summer festival while Samhain was the time of the Winter festival. Human sacrifice was offered at both festivals. According to Julius Caesar[4] in his *Commentaries,* and other sources, the Celts believed they were descended from the god *Dis,* a tradition handed down from the Druids. Dis was the Roman name for the god of the dead.

Of the 400 names of Celtic gods known, Belenus is mentioned most often. "Samhain" as the specific name of the Lord of Death is uncertain, but it is possible that the Lord of Death was the chief druidic deity. We'll follow the lead of several other authors and call him Samhain.

The Celts and their Druid priests began their New Year on November 1, which marked the beginning of Winter. They apparently believed that on October 31, the night before their New Year and the last day of the old year, the Lord of Death gathered the souls of the evil dead who had been condemned to enter the bodies of animals. He then decided what animal form they would take for the next year. (The souls of the good dead were reincarnated as humans.) The Druids also believed that the punishment of the evil dead could be lightened by sacrifices, prayers and gifts to the Lord of Death.

Druid worshipers attempted to placate and appease the Lord of Death because of his power over the souls of the dead, whether these souls were good or evil. For those who had died during the proceeding 12 months, Samhain allowed their spirits to return to earth to their former places of habitation for a few hours to associate once again with their families.[5]

Thus, the Celts believed that on their New Year's Eve (our Halloween) ghosts, evil spirits and, some say, witches roamed about. In order to honor the Sun God (Belenus), and to frighten away evil spirits who allegedly feared fire, large bonfires were lit on hilltops. In Lewis Spence's *The History and Origins of Druidism* we read,

> The outstanding feature of *Samhain* was the burning of a great fire....*Samhain* was also a festival of the dead, whose spirits at this season were thought of as scouring the countryside, causing dread to the folk at large. To expel them from the fields and the precincts of villages, lighted brands from the bonfire were carried around the district...divinations for the fate of the individual throughout the new year were engaged in (page 99).

For several days before New Year's Eve, young boys would travel the neighborhood begging material for the great bonfires. The fires were believed to not only banish evil spirits but to rejuvenate the sun. Until fairly recent times, the hilltop Halloween fires of the Scotts were called *Samhnagan*, indicating the lingering influence of the ancient Celtic festival.[6]

On this night, evil or frustrated ghosts were also supposed to play tricks on humans and to cause supernatural manifestations. As part of the celebration, people donned grotesque masks and danced around the great bonfires often pretending they were being pursued by evil spirits. And while these bonfires were lit to scare away evil spirits, food was put out to make the ghosts or souls of the good dead that Samhain had released feel welcome and at home.

Because Samhain marked the beginning of a new year, an interest in divination and fortune-telling became an important part of this holiday. For example, the Druids believed that the particular shape of various fruits and vegetables could divine the future. Victims of human sacrifice were used for the same purpose. When the Romans conquered Britain, some of their customs were added to those of the Druids while others, such as human sacrifice, were banned.

Of course, the Samhain celebration was not unique. Many festivals worldwide celebrate a time when the dead return to mingle with the living. The Hindus have their night of Holi. The Iroquois Indians celebrate a Feast of the Dead every 12 years, when all those who have died during the 12 years are honored with prayers. A national holiday in Mexico, the Day of the Dead, begins on November 2 and lasts several days. In this gruesome festival, death becomes a kind of neighborly figure, appearing on candy, jewelry, toys, bread, cakes, and so on. This is the time when the souls of the dead return and when the living are to honor them: for example, doors are decorated with flowers to welcome the *Angelitos*, the souls of dead children.

One study of festivals and special days points out that Halloween "rivals St. John's Eve for omens, spells and all sorts of mystic practices, which, in its case, are connected with the waning power of the sun and with the great druidical festival of Samhain."[7]

For the most part, then, our modern Halloween appears to initially be traced to the practices of the ancient Druids at their Winter festival on October 31.

2. Are the specific customs of Halloween related to pagan beliefs?

Since Halloween itself originated with paganism, it is hardly surprising that its customs are related to pagan belief. According to the *Encyclopedia Britannica,*

> In ancient Britain and Ireland, the Celtic Festival of Samhain was observed on October 31, at the end of summer.... The souls of the dead were supposed to revisit their homes on this day and the autumnal festival acquired sinister significance, with ghosts, witches, goblins, black cats, fairies and demons of all kinds said to be roaming about. It was the time to placate the supernatural powers controlling the processes of nature. In addition, Halloween was thought to be the most favorable time for divinations concerning marriage, luck, health, and death. It was the only day on which the help of the devil was invoked for such purposes.[8]

Halloween symbols, customs and practices undoubtedly have had a variety of influences upon them historically. For example, in early American history Halloween was not practiced nor is it primarily an English or Protestant holiday. It was not widely observed until the twentieth century. Initially, it was only practiced in small Irish Catholic settlements until thousands of Irishmen migrated here during the great potato famine and brought their customs with them. To some degree, our modern Halloween is an Irish holiday in origin going back to the Celtic festival. (Ireland is the only place in the world where Halloween is actually a national holiday.) Coincidentally, the rise in popularity of Halloween in America coincides roughly with the national spiritist revival that began in 1848.[9]

Among the modern customs and practices of Halloween, we note the following probable or possible influences.

The Jack-o'-lantern. The carved pumpkin may have originated with the witches' use of a skull with a candle in it to light the way to coven meetings. But among the Irish, who, as noted, caused the popularization of Halloween in America, the legend of "Irish Jack" explains the jack-o'-lantern. The legend goes: There was a stingy drunk named Jack who tricked the devil into climbing an apple tree for an apple but then cut the sign of a cross into the trunk of the tree preventing the devil from coming down. Jack forced the devil to swear he would never come after Jack's soul. The devil reluctantly agreed. Jack eventually died but was turned away at the gates of heaven because of his drunkenness and life of selfishness. He was next sent to the devil who also rejected him, keeping his promise. Since Jack had no place to go, he was condemned to wander the earth. As he was leaving hell (he happened to be eating a turnip), the devil threw a live coal at him. He put the coal inside the turnip and has since forever been roaming the earth with his "jack-o'-lantern" in search of a place to rest. Eventually, pumpkins replaced turnips since it was much easier to symbolize the devil's coal inside a pumpkin.

Trick-or-Treat and Halloween Costumes. There are several possibilities for the origin of this pastime. One is from the idea that witches allegedly had to steal the materials needed for their festivals. The ancient Druids may have believed that witches held this day to be special, something clearly true for modern witches.

The idea of trick-or-treating is further related to the ghosts of the dead in pagan, and even Catholic, history. For example, among the ancient Druids, "The ghosts that were thought to throng about the houses of the living were greeted with a banquet-laden table. At the end of the feast, masked and costumed villagers representing the souls of the dead paraded to the outskirts of town leading the ghosts away."[10]

As noted, Halloween was a night where mischievous and evil spirits roamed freely. As in modern poltergeist lore, mischievous spirits could play tricks on the living—so it was advantageous to "hide" from them by wearing costumes. Masks and costumes were worn to either scare away the ghosts or keep from being recognized by them: "In Ireland especially, people thought that ghosts and spirits roamed after dark on Halloween. They lit candles or lanterns to keep the spirits away, and if they had to go outside, they wore costumes and masks to frighten the spirits or to keep from being recognized by these unearthly beings."[11]

Halloween masks and costumes may also be related to the attempt to hide one's attendance at pagan festivals or, as in traditional shamanism and other forms of animism, to change the personality of the wearer to allow for communication with the spirit world. Here, costumes could be worn to ward off evil spirits. Or the costume wearer might even absorb the power of the animal represented by the mask and costume worn. Thus, Halloween costumes may have originated with the Celtic Druid ceremonial participants who wore animal heads and skins to acquire the strength of the particular animal.

Another possible explanation for costuming originates with the medieval Catholic practice of displaying the relics of the saints on All Saints Day: "The poorer churches could not afford relics and so instituted a procession with parishioners dressed as the patron saints; the extras dressed as angels or devils and everyone paraded around the churchyard."[12]

Going from door to door seeking treats may hail back to the Druid practice of begging material for the great bonfires. As we will see later, it is also related to the Catholic concept of purgatory and the custom of begging for a "soul cake."

As for the "trick" custom of Halloween, this is related to the idea that ghosts and witches created mischief on this particular night. For example, if the living did not provide food or "treats" for the spirits, then they would "trick" the living. People feared that terrible things might happen to them if they did not honor the spirits. The Druids also believed that failure to worship their gods would bring dire consequences: If the gods were not treated properly in ritual, they would seek vengeance. Further, some people soon realized that a mischievous sense of humor could be camouflaged—that they could perform practical jokes on others and blame it on the ghosts or witches roaming about.

Fruits and nuts. Halloween involves fruit centerpieces, apples and nuts. Three of the sacred fruits of the Celts were acorns, apples and nuts, especially the hazelnut, considered a god, and the acorn, sacred from its association to the oak. Fruits and nuts also seem to be related to the Roman Harvest Feast of Pomona. For example, in ancient Rome, cider was drawn and the Romans bobbed for apples. Dunking for apples became an aspect of romance divination for discovering your future mate.

Telling ghost stories. Because Halloween was a night where dead souls were believed to be everywhere, and good, mischievous and evil spirits roamed freely, the custom of telling ghost stories on Halloween originated as a natural consequences of such beliefs.

3. How does Halloween relate historically to the Catholic Church, the dead and purgatory?

In the Middle Ages the Catholic Church attempted to oppose the paganism involved in the Samhain festival by making November 1 All Saint's Day and November 2 All Soul's Day. As noted, All Saint's Day was a celebration of the saints, especially the ones that were martyrs. All Soul's Day became a day to pray for the dead and to help them escape the torments of purgatory.

On May 13 in the year 609 or 610, Pope Boniface IV dedicated the Roman Pantheon to the Virgin Mary and all the Christian martyrs. In 835 Pope Gregory IV transferred this feast of All Saints to November 1 and extended it to include all the saints.[13] So November 1, All Saint's Day, the day after Halloween (Hallow's Eve or All Saint's Eve), became a day dedicated by the Catholic Church to the Virgin Mary and the saints. Eventually, November 2 became All Soul's Day as a special day to pray for the dead. As we will see, this custom originated with a supernatural vision of the Catholic Saint Odilo, who died in 1048.

Reminiscent of the ancient Druids, the Catholic Church still teaches that the living may, through various acts, alleviate the sufferings of the dead. They may pray for the souls being tormented in purgatory and ease their pains through specific or sacrificial acts such as penance, partaking of the Sacraments, mortification, using the Rosary, and good deeds like almsgiving. Prayers are especially to be said to the Virgin Mary, who is believed to have the power to release the suffering from purgatory. (This Catholic concept of purgatory also has many parallels in other religions, but the idea is neither biblical nor Christian.[see note 14] The distressing consequences of this false belief is illustrated in books like Fr. F.X. Shouppe, *Purgatory: Explained by the Lives and Legends of the Saints.*[15])

The Catholic Saint Odilo was Abbot of Clugny. He had a vision, perhaps, like many Catholic saints or mystics, of souls suffering terribly in purgatory. This vision inspired him to have special masses said on their behalf in all the churches affiliated with Clugny and the practice soon spread.[16] As an article in *U.S. Catholic* observes, "By the end of the 13th century, All Soul's Day on November 2nd had become a set feast day to pray for our dead throughout the Latin church."[17] The article points out that Halloween, All Saint's Day and All Soul's Day are days to concentrate on, in this order: sin, sanctification, and the dead:[18]

> And on November 2, All Soul's Day, let's hope some people will go to the cemetery or to a church and pray for us, their dead. Halloween, All Saint's Day, All Soul's Day—October 31st, November 1st, November 2nd—all are feast days and All Saint's Day is a holy day of obligation. We must admit that we are sinners, that we are obliged to honor the saints and are called to be saints ourselves, and that it is our duty to remember our dead, the faithful departed.[19]

As noted, the ancient Druids believed in a purgatory-like concept: "The Celts believed that the sinful souls of those who had died during the year had been relegated to the bodies of animals. Through gifts and sacrifices their sins could be expiated and the souls freed to claim a heavenly reward. Samhain judged the souls and decreed in what form their existence was to continue, whether in the body of a human being or in an animal."[20] Let's consider other historic and contemporary examples of how Halloween and purgatory are related.

In the late 1800s, it was customary for English Catholics to assemble at midnight on Halloween and pray for the souls of their departed friends. "The custom was observed in every Catholic farm in the district, but was gradually given up."[21] One individual reported in November 1909 that his grandfather would light a bundle of straw and throw it into the air with his pitchfork; short prayers were said while the straw was lit and thrown. When asked about it "my grandfather replied that it was to represent the holy souls escaping from Purgatory to Heaven."[22]

On November 2 in Belgium, people eat special "All Soul's" cakes because, supposedly, "the more cakes you eat on this night, the more souls you can save from Purgatory."[23] "In Sicily, on All Soul's Day, cakes with images of skulls and skeletons are eaten."[24] A popular Halloween song in the Philippines goes, ". . . ordinary souls we are, from Purgatory we have come. And there we are duty-bound to pray by night and day. If alms you are to give, be in a hurry please for the door of heaven may close on us forever."[25] In France, All Soul's Day (*Le Jour des Morts*) "is dedicated to prayers for the dead who are not yet glorified."[26]

Ruth Hutchison and Ruth Adams report that in earlier times people took special bread called "souls" to the cemeteries, placing it on the graves. The people ate these "soul cakes" because they were thought to be a powerful antidote against any flames of purgatory "that might be invoked by returning ghosts. At dusk the festival changed from All Saint's Day to All Soul's Eve. Lighted candles were placed on graves and in windows, to guide the dead back home."[27] In the Middle Ages on All Soul's Day, the poor would go begging for soul cakes which could be given as payment for prayers they had promised to say for the dead.[28]

These examples illustrate how Halloween is related both to ancient Celtic practice and the Catholic concept of purgatory. Significantly, the Lutheran Church observes October 31, or the Sunday nearest it, as the beginning of the

Protestant Reformation. In Martin Luther's time, the corrupt practice of buying indulgences for the dead "suffering in purgatory" was common. Appropriately, in 1517, Luther nailed his 95 theses, which attacked the concept of indulgences, on the Castle Church door (in Wittenberg, Germany) on Halloween day itself.[29]

4. Is Halloween related to modern occult practices?

Although Halloween as commonly practiced today is an innocent time for most youngsters, it is a very serious observance for many witches, neo-pagans and other occultists. Before we proceed, it should be noted that the historic and contemporary occult associations to Halloween have produced something of a "crossover" effect to the larger society so that in some instances the observance of Halloween is not necessarily an innocent practice. Reading through various histories of Halloween one is struck at the large number of superstitions and divinatory practices involved. Some of the former (and all the latter) can be related to the occult.

Of concern is how superstitions may regulate or control one's life in unsavory ways. Further, true divinatory practices are almost always consequential, as we discussed in our *Encyclopedia of New Age Beliefs* (Harvest House Publishers, 1996). Indeed, since the last quarter of the ninteenth century Halloween has been regarded as a time "for working charms, spells, and divinations."[30] As we've noted before, this may be related to the ancient Druids since Samhain marked the beginning of the new year, which resulted in an interest in divination and fortune-telling to ascertain what the coming year would bring.

On Halloween, it was believed (and still is in some places) that following a particular ritual may allow an apparition of one's future mate to appear behind you: "Many beliefs arose about how to conjure up the image of one's future wife or husband. Girls believed that if one sat at midnight before a mirror eating an apple, the image of her future husband would suddenly appear before her. If no image appeared it was taken to mean that the girl would remain a spinster."[31] In Ireland, "on Hallow Eve Night the spirits of the dead rise and go on the earth, girls at the hearth play at divining the identities of future mates, and in the past boys dressed in suits of white straw and caroused over the hills in the company of the dead, attacking the homes of men who kept their daughters from the cohort of bachelors."[32] Others believe "an apple peeling thrown over the left shoulder will curve into the initial of the one you will marry."[33] In Scotland, "if a girl went into her room at midnight on the fatal eve [Halloween] and sat down before her mirror and cut an apple into nine slices and held each slice on the point of her knife before eating it she might see in the mirror looking over her shoulder the face of her future lover and he would ask for the last slice."[34] As we've noted, the use of fruits and nuts for divination on Halloween was borrowed from the Celts and Romans.[35] In fact, "The use of nuts for divination was so common that even in America Halloween was once known as 'Nutcrack Night.'"[36]

Halloween is also a common day for children to pull out a Ouija board and attempt to contact the ghosts and spirits that are believed to be roaming about. But as we documented in our *Encyclopedia of New Age Beliefs*, Ouija boards are anything but an innocent pastime and may lead to such serious consequences as mental illness or spirit-possession.

Divination concerning one's death was and is practiced on Halloween. On Halloween in North Wales, every family built a large bonfire near their house. The fire, termed Coel Coeth, became a means of divination. Each member of the house would throw a white stone into the fire having marked it for later identification. In the morning they returned to the ashes in search of their stones. "If any stone was missing, the Welshman believed that its owner would not live to see another Halloween."[37]

Others believed that if one ate a crust of dry bread before going to bed on Halloween, his wish would be fulfilled.[38]

In the southern United States, there is a custom based on the Druidic belief (see page 16) that the struggles of victims of human sacrifice revealed omens of the future: "Alcohol was put in a bowl and lighted and 'fortunes' in the shape of figs, orange peel, raisins, almonds and dates, wrapped in tin foil were thrown into the flame. The girl who snatched out of the burning the best thing would meet her future husband within a year."[39] Under the subheading of "Halloween Charms," one popular book for children gives a description of British customs involving rituals for divining different aspects of one's future.[40]

The concern over such activities can be seen in the following statement from the *American Book of Days*: "Various methods of divining the future were used on Halloween and the results were accepted in all seriousness."[41] In other words, when we are dealing with a sober approach to divining the future—with subjects such as overall fortune, marriage partners, or life and death—the consequences in people's lives may be much more than mere games.

Today, other occult practices are found on Halloween. In New Orleans, "The Voodoo Museum usually offers a special Halloween ritual in which people may see true voodoo rites."[42] And in Salem, Massachusetts, a Halloween festival occurs from October 13 to 31 and includes a psychic fair.[43]

In contemporary witchcraft, Halloween is also considered a special night. A standard book on neo-paganism reports the following as the key celebration days of witchcraft: "The greater sabbats are: *Samhain* (Halloween or November Eve), the Celtic New Year; the days when the walls between the worlds were said to be thinnest and when contact with one's ancestors took place; *Oimelc* (February 1), the winter purification festival . . . *Beltane* (May 1), the great fertility festival . . . different Craft traditions . . . treat the festivals in diverse ways. But almost all traditions at least celebrate Samhain and Beltane."[44] Some witches even request a day off from work for their special day while others have actually sought to have schools closed to commemorate their great sabbat.

Many satanic groups also consider Halloween a special night in part because Halloween "became the only day of the year in which it was believed that the devil could be invoked for help in finding out about future marriages, health, deaths, crops, and what was to happen in the near year."[45] Indeed, witchcraft and satanism share certain other commonalities.[see note 46] Although they are distinct entities, and, even allowing for a qualified legitimacy to the modern neo-pagan claim of disdain for satanism per se, there remains clear biblical precedent that the devil is the source of power behind witchcraft and all forms of the occult.[47] Former witch Doreen Irvine observes, "Witchcraft of the black kind is not far removed from satanism. . . . Black witches have great power and are not to be taken lightly. . . . They [may] exhume fresh graves and offer the bodies in sacrifice to Satan."[48]

In addition, there are human sacrifices that take place in certain satanist and neo-pagan groups. Human sacrifice also occurred regularly among the Druids. According to Roman historian Tacitus, the Druids "covered their altars with the blood" of victims, mostly criminals; according to Caesar, human sacrifice was a common and frequent element in Druidism. In large cages scores of people were burned alive at once; the larger the number of victims, the greater the yield of crops.[49] But if the gods were not appeased by the sacrifice of criminals, innocent victims were also offered. (According to Lucan, a first century Latin poet, in his *Pharsalia*, three Celt gods in particular were hungry for human souls—Teutates, Esus and Taranis.[50]) We noted earlier that the struggles of the dying victims were held to contain predictions of the future. The Druids had full confidence in human sacrifice as a method of divination. According to Spence, "Horrible indeed was the method by which the Druids divined future events after a human sacrifice. 'The Druids,' says Tacitus, 'consult the gods in the palpitating entrails of men,' while Strabo informs us that they stabbed a human victim in the back with a sword and then drew omens from the convulsive movements made by him in his death-struggles. Diodorus says that they augured from the posture in which the victim fell, from his contortions, and the direction in which the blood flowed from the body. From these, 'they formed their predictions according to certain rules left them by their ancestors.'"[51]

We will discuss the relationship between witchcraft and Halloween later. However, the above material indicates that Halloween of past and present can be much more than merely a day of children's trick or treating.

Section II
A Christian and Biblical Analysis of Halloween

5. Do pagan elements of Halloween automatically disqualify it for Christian participation?

So far we have examined Halloween from the perspective of history and paganism. Does our discussion lead us to conclude that Halloween is off-limits for Christians?

On the one hand, we would not deny that because of the modern occult revival and its implications for society, one must strongly question the advisability of Christian parents allowing their children to dress up as genuine occult characters, such as witches, Satanists, wizards, Druids, or to dress in any manner that could bring dishonor to our Lord. As we documented in *The Coming Darkness* (Harvest House Publishers, 1993), the occult is anything but a harmless pastime, and to associate one's child with it, even indirectly in humor or jest, is probably unwise. And, as we will see later, God is very clear about not being associated with the occult.

On the other hand, the contemporary practice of Halloween is hardly unique in sporting remnants of paganism. Such remnants can be found in many American holidays and customs. It would be difficult to argue that participation in all these holidays must be rejected merely because of pagan associations historically. It is evident that the pagan remnants of the practice of Halloween and other holidays no longer carry the meaning they once had to most people. Christmas, Easter and other holidays were all derived from pagan celebrations that the church appropriated and depaganized or made Christian—as is true for Halloween.

For example, the Christmas tree apparently originates from the ancient European idea that the evergreen tree embodied powerful spirits; Easter involved a pagan fertility ritual. The practice of sending cards on Valentine's Day may go back to the characteristically licentious Roman feast of Lupercalia. The custom of kissing someone under a mistletoe branch can be traced to ancient druidic beliefs concerning its sexual potency (hence their reverence for the plant); fertility rites and sacrifices were also associated with mistletoe. Birthday cakes probably originated from offering candles and cakes to Artemis, the ancient Greek goddess of the moon and hunt. The idea of June brides is related to Juno, the Roman goddess of marriage, who presided over the month of June. In fact, most aspects of the American wedding ceremony can be traced to ancient pagan customs—including the bride's white dress and veil, exchanging of wedding rings, and the father giving the bride away. Should we avoid weddings merely because of its "pagan" elements? The answer, of course, is no.

The custom of passing out cigars at a baby's birth may come from the ancient Mayan fathers who would blow tobacco smoke toward the sun god as a fragrant offering of thanks for their child. Our own childhood episodes involving the "tooth fairy" may be related to the attempt to hide physical items from practitioners of voodoo who would use such items for their cursing rituals. Even the days of the week are named after pagan gods: for example, Thursday refers to "Thor's day"; Wednesday refers to "Woden's day"; Saturday refers to "Saturn's day," Monday is moon day.

Although the remnants of ancient paganism persist, the anti-Christian beliefs and practices once associated with Christmas, Easter, Valentine's Day and other holidays and customs long ago vanished. Thus, would anyone argue it is wrong to celebrate Christmas in honor of Christ's birth and give gifts to loved ones as a reflection of the loving gift God has given to us in Jesus—merely because Christmas was *once* a pagan holiday or because it remains a pagan (or materialistic) holiday in various places around the world?

In similar fashion, even in spite of its occult associations today, the manner in which people use Halloween should determine our attitude toward it. We cannot logically condemn what is, for most people, a purely secular pastime that can be engaged in without any occult associations at all.

6. What biblical principles apply for discerning this issue?

We have shown some of the reasons why there is a controversy over the issue of Halloween. If we lived back in the 1940s or 50s, when the world of the occult was still largely in the closet and Halloween was a far more innocent activity, there would be little debate over participation. The concern some Christians have, in light of our culture's turn toward the occult, is whether it is still acceptable to participate in an activity that has some degree of association with the occult. Below we offer some scriptural and other guidelines.

First, it should be recognized that the occult activities and phenomena we have discussed so far are still largely removed from the activity of mainstream Halloween celebrations. No one should be concerned that they are "supporting the occult" by dressing their child as a bunny rabbit for trick or treating. Any real occult activities that may be associated with Halloween in the larger community can easily be avoided. If a teacher at school has children or students studying the occult to understand the historical background of Halloween, has guest lecturers who are occultists, or is in any way interesting or encouraging children toward the occult, parents have the legal right to remove their child from such potentially consequential activities and express their concerns to their teachers.

Second, we must carefully evaluate the circumstances involved, as well as allow and respect the differences of opinion on this subject. The apostle Paul's discussion of circumstantial prohibition, individual conscience, and personal conviction in 1 Corinthians 10:18-29, Romans 14:1-13, and elsewhere is to the point.

In his own time, the apostle Paul knew that eating food—even food previously sacrificed to pagan idols—had no spiritual significance in itself. But there were also times when such food was to be avoided. When a Christian actually ate food *at* a pagan temple, food that was just offered in sacrifice and worship to pagan gods—gods that were really demons—the apostle prohibited this because of the unavoidable direct associations and implications. To eat such food was to also be involved in the worship of pagan gods and, hence, idolatrous, a violation of the first and second commandments.

Also, whenever a Christian did something in the presence of a weaker brother that caused him to stumble, Paul prohibited this. Let's briefly examine his teachings in detail.

The apostle Paul knew that an idol was nothing and that there was no actual god associated with the idol. He knew that demons, not gods, were the unseen objects behind idol worship. Therefore, in his first argument in 1 Corinthians 10, he warns God's people that if they did eat meat sacrificed to idols they should *not* eat it with pagans *in their temples* because then they would become "participants with demons":

> Consider the people of Israel: Do not those who eat the sacrifices participate in the altar? Do I mean then that a sacrifice offered to an idol is anything, or that an idol is anything? No, but the sacrifices of pagans are offered to demons, not to God, and I do not want you to be participants with demons. You cannot drink the cup of the Lord and the cup of demons too; you cannot have a part in both the Lord's table and the table of demons. (1 Corinthians 10:18-21).

That which *is* sacrificed is unavoidably related to that *for which* it is sacrificed. "When the people of Israel ate part of the sacrifice made at the altar (Leviticus 7:15; 8:31; Deuteronomy 12:17-18), they participated in the worship of God, who established the sacrifices and whose altar it was."[52] Thus, the apostle knew that to participate in the ritual observances associated with feasting was to participate *in the worship* of the actual spiritual reality behind the altar. In the case of Israel, it involved the one true God; in the case of the pagans, it involved demons. Therefore, it was impossible to actively participate in pagan feasts in their temples without participating with demons. Since all the gods of the Gentile world were really demons, the essence of idolatry was seen to be demon worship and, for the apostle Paul, this was certainly something to be avoided.

The Scripture is clear that there is only one true God (See Isaiah 44:6,8; 46:9). So, it is logical to conclude there is only one true religion. Therefore Scripture is correct when it declares "all the gods of the nations are idols" (Psalm 96:5). Further, if Scripture teaches that the spiritual power and reality behind idols involves demons (1 Corinthians 10:20;

Psalm 106:37), then all idolatry and all false religion are by definition involved in demon worship—whether the participants realize it or not (Acts 26:18). Hence Paul's concern.

But the apostle Paul argues that it was another thing entirely to eat meat sacrificed to idols *after* it had been brought to the marketplace and purchased. For those mature in the faith, such meat had no spiritual significance. Only when someone was present whose conscience was violated because he could not eat such meat in faith was there a legitimate issue to be decided. At this point, we are to defer to that person and not stand in judgment upon him.

Thus, in the second part of Paul's argument in 1 Corinthians 10, his concern is that we not violate the conscience of a weaker brother or sister and therefore cause them to sin in their own mind:

> "Everything is permissible"—but not everything is beneficial. "Everything is permissible"—but not everything is constructive. Nobody should seek his own good, but the good of others. Eat anything sold in the meat market without raising questions of conscience, for, "the earth is the Lord's, and everything in it." If some unbeliever invites you to a meal and you want to go, eat whatever is put before you without raising questions of conscience. But if anyone says to you, "this has been offered in [pagan] sacrifice," then do not eat it, both for the sake of the man who told you and for conscience's sake—the other man's conscience, I mean, not yours. For why should my freedom be judged by another's conscience?" (1 Corinthians 10:23-29).

In New Testament times, there were other matters in which Christians had different views on besides meat sacrificed to idols. For example, Jewish Christians may have been unwilling to give up certain requirements of the law such as dietary restrictions, the Sabbath or other special days. The apostle Paul responded as follows,

> Accept him whose faith is weak, without passing judgment on disputable matters. One man's faith allows him to eat everything, but another man whose faith is weak, eats only vegetables.... One man considers one day more sacred than another; another man considers every day alike. Each one should be fully convinced in his own mind.... Therefore let us stop passing judgment on one another. Instead, make up your mind not to put any stumbling block or obstacle in your brother's way (Romans 14:1,2,5,13).

How does this relate to Halloween? In the same way. When a person believes their conscience will be violated by participating in *any* form of Halloween activity, and when they cannot do so in faith, then no one else should look down upon them or be their judge. Let's paraphrase and apply Romans 14:3, "The man who participates in Halloween must not look down on him who does not, and the man who does not participate in Halloween must not condemn the man who does, for God has accepted him."

In Romans 14:1, Paul says that we are speaking of "disputable matters," matters of *individual* perception and faith—not matters of essential doctrine or morality. Therefore, neither the one who participates in Halloween nor the one who doesn't should judge the other. The apostle Paul wrote, "Therefore do not let anyone judge you by what you eat or drink, or with regard to a religious festival, a New Moon celebration or a Sabbath day" (Colossians 2:16). He also wrote "everything that does not come from faith is sin" (Romans 14:23), and further, "As one who is in the Lord Jesus, I am fully convinced that no food is unclean in itself. But if anyone regards something as unclean, then for him it is unclean. If your brother is distressed because of what you eat, you are no longer acting in love.... Do not allow what you consider good to be spoken of as evil" (Romans 14:14-16).

In other words, if you are going to participate in Halloween, exercise discernment with your Christian friends. Do not invite a family who would be offended to your house and encourage their children to go out "trick or treating" with yours.

Besides the issue of those who don't want anything to do with Halloween because of its occult history and contemporary occult associations, there is the issue of those who are converted out of the occult or may have participated in evil activities on Halloween. Certainly we should respect the wishes of such individuals and be careful not to dredge up what may be a truly painful past.

In Scripture we are told that the spiritual man judges all things and that, in the future, we will actually judge angels. If so, then we are clearly competent to judge trivial matters now (1 Corintians 2:15; 6:3). If we test everything, hold on to the good and avoid every kind of evil, we will fulfill our obligations (1 Thessalonians 5:21,22). By examining this issue carefully and respecting the convictions of others, we will arrive at a biblical position regarding Halloween.

However, when Halloween activities actually involve genuine occult practices, the Scripture is clear that these are to be avoided. Both the Old and New Testaments have many references condemning the practice of witchcraft, sorcery, spiritism, contacting the dead, divination, and so forth—all things *potentially* associated with Halloween.

> Do not turn to mediums or seek out spiritists, for you will be defiled by them. I am the LORD your God (Leviticus 19:31).

> Let no one be found among you who sacrifices his son or daughter in the fire, who practices divination or sorcery, interprets omens, engages in witchcraft, or casts spells, or who is a medium or spiritist or who consults the dead.... The nations you will dispossess listen to those who practice sorcery or divination. But as for you, the Lord your God has not permitted you to do so (Deuteronomy 18:10, 11, 14).

> [King Manasseh of Judah] practiced sorcery, divination and witchcraft, and consulted mediums and spiritists. He did much evil in the eyes of the LORD, provoking him to anger (2 Chronicles 33:6).

Nowhere are we told such activities are acceptable before God. In light of these scriptures, no one can logically argue that the Bible is accepting of such practices.

7. What are some Halloween alternatives?

There are many positive alternatives to Halloween. No child should feel left out because his parents don't want him to participate in the traditional observances. Many churches have alternative activities on Halloween night such as "carnivals" and youth parties. Halloween may also be made into a special family get-together of a party and games at home. At church or home, individuals may come dressed as either Bible characters or important individuals in church history, American history, and so on. You may also have a special time of prayer during the party where youths are encouraged to pray for their friends at school, their families, or even for people involved in the occult on this day, so they, too, might find salvation. Pray also that God will stop what is already a highly consequential occult revival in our land. And certainly, for the children who come knocking at the door, parents might wish to give, in addition to candy, a briefly written age-appropriate message on salvation— especially if it has been creatively written to tie it to the season. Halloween can be both a fun time and spiritually productive for all concerned. (For practical advice on Halloween, see page 43.)

We have examined Halloween historically and in the present and concluded that with proper attention to Scripture, conscience and commonsense, observance of Halloween as an innocent pastime is up to the individual. But we are not through with the subject of Halloween. Halloween is also associated with real occult activity and we would be amiss to leave this out.

Section III
Halloween, Haunted Houses, Poltergeists and Witchcraft

8. *What is the historic connection between Halloween and ghosts? Are "Halloween ghosts" only myths?*

From its origins with the ancient Druids and their cult of death,[53] the dominant theme of Halloween has been one of ghosts, spirits and the dead. Lewis Spence reports, "There is no doubt that the original idea underlying all these various ceremonials is that the spirits of the dead might be pacified and prevented from haunting the living. The festivals to the dead are among the earliest in the world . . . beginning with the idea of fear, and therefore of propitiation. . . . "[54] Indeed, the degree of influence of the spirits of the dead, ghosts and poltergeists upon Halloween and related festivals around the world can be seen in literature and the media.

The influence of the supposed ghosts of the human dead on Halloween and, in fact, most religious traditions throughout the world, takes us to our next section. As we've noted, Halloween may be an innocent pastime, but some of the practices and phenomena associated with Halloween need to be carefully evaluated and taken seriously. We hope the reader will understand that although we first chose a more lighthearted subject to discuss, we are now evaluating a far more sober phenomenon routinely associated with it. By its historical associations and very nature, Halloween can lead people to a fascination with things like the phenomenon of poltergeists and genuine witchcraft. We examine these in turn.

9. *How are ghosts, haunted houses and Halloween related?*

> The poltergeist is something that must be fought as well as investigated.[55]
>
> — The late psychical researcher, D. Scott Rogo

Ghosts, things that go bump in the night, spooks, poltergeists, haunted houses. Halloween aside, ghost stories are everywhere today. Literally dozens of TV specials and segments on programs like "Unsolved Mysteries," "The 'X' Files," "Sightings," "The Extraordinary" and "Paranormal Borderline" captivate millions of onlookers. Haunted houses are even in demand and some realtors specialize in selling them to fascinated clients—at greatly inflated prices. (One wonders if they get their money's worth.)

Every Halloween, television programmers market an interesting lineup of supernatural thrillers on TV. Although Halloween comes and goes, interest in the intriguing phenomenon of the ghost or poltergeist remains all year long. Poltergeists have also found their way into immensely popular movies on ghosts such as "Ghost Dad" with Bill Cosby, "Ghost" with Patrick Swayze, and "Ghost Busters."

The term poltergeist comes from two German words: *polter*, to make noise by throwing or tumbling around, and *geist*, ghost or spirit. The literal translation of the term is "noisy ghost."

These "noisy ghosts" are nothing new. Michael Goss compiled an annotated bibliography of over 1,000 English books on poltergeists from the last century alone (1880-1970). In his text he observes, "Poltergeists seem to have been plaguing the human race since the dawn of time and they have shown a grand impartiality as to the theatres of their operations. They are as much at home in the jungles of Indonesia as they are in the suburbs of London or the bustle of New York City."[56] Indeed, throughout America, "Poltergeist experiences occur every day of the week."[57] Hardly anyone hasn't heard genuine ghost stories, but even among the millions who have personally experienced ghosts, few have any real idea as to what is actually going on.

10. What are the theories advanced to explain ghosts?

The theories put forth to explain or identify ghosts or poltergeists are almost as diverse as the phenomenon itself. Among those advanced are that poltergeists are 1) the spirits of human dead; 2) unknown spirits; 3) demonic spirits or biblical demons; 4) spontaneous, uncontrollable outbursts of supposed psychokinetic energy, usually associated with a young person emerging into adolescence; 5) various other manifestations of alleged human psychic activity; 6) inexplicable phenomena resulting from unknown, strange geophysical conditions (although this view is held by some noted rationalistically inclined psychic investigators, it is perhaps the least credible theory to those who have personally experienced poltergeist events); 7) consequences of the human spirit being projected or forced outside the body as in uncontrollable out-of-body experiences or "astral" projection; and 8) a post-mortum "vestige" of human personality somehow imbued with powers to affect the physical realm.

The three most common theories are: 1) the Christian view that poltergeists are biblical demons; 2) the mediumistic interpretation that poltergeists are the roaming spirits of the human dead; and 3) the parapsychological view that poltergeists constitute an entirely human phenomenon and result from various manifestations of alleged psychic, i.e., psychokinetic, power.

Note that the last two interpretations justify certain pre-existing theories which are often passionately advocated by those who hold them. Thus, in the mediumistic view, poltergeists provide alleged evidence that all spirits of the human dead may roam freely—and, thus, are not immediately confined to heaven or hell as the Bible teaches (see Matthew 25:46; Luke 16:16-30; 2 Peter 2:9; Revelation 20:10-15). This supports the occult belief that men and women never die spiritually in the biblical sense of eternal separation from God. Rather, it is believed that, in general, the spirits of the human dead merely experience a normal transition into the next life where they have the opportunity to continue their spiritual evolution based on individual merit earned in their previous life (or lives). This interpretation of ghosts is often incorporated with belief in reincarnation.

The parapsychological view interprets poltergeists in a different manner. Poltergeist phenomena are believed to result from an alleged recurrent spontaneous psychokinesis (RSPK) of adolescents (usually females), that is, from the alleged psychic powers of the human mind. This idea lends support to the cherished theory of innate human psychic potential long advocated by the parapsychological and New Age communities. For example, in ascribing poltergeist phenomena to human psychic power, the late noted psychical researcher D. Scott Rogo comments, "In thinking about man's unwelcomed guests, the poltergeists, let us remember that our psychic abilities can plague as well as benefit us."[58] However, some psychical researchers have also accepted the occult, mediumistic interpretation that these entities are "troubled or confused" ghosts or "earthbound spirits" who, because of their past life or lives on earth, have been hampered in their spiritual "evolution." Rather than progress into higher spirit realms or the "finer" dimensions of the spiritual world, they remain aggressively attached to the "earth plane."

We find these last two theories unconvincing in light of both biblical revelation and the nature and actions of the poltergeist itself. We reject the mediumistic theory because the Bible teaches the human dead are either with Christ in heaven or confined to punishment in hell—and therefore unable to roam in the spirit world and/or haunt houses (see Philippians 1:23; 2 Corinthians 5:6-8; Luke 16:22-26; 2 Peter 2:9). We reject the parapsychological theory because we believe the idea that human beings have genuine psychic powers is largely a myth. We document this in our book, *Cult Watch* (Harvest House Publishers, 1991, pp. 257-81).

So how do we explain real ghosts?

11. Is the Christian view of ghosts credible in light of the facts surrounding hauntings and poltergeists?

The Christian view explains poltergeist phenomena as the result of the activities of demons. But is this theory really credible? Most serious researchers will hardly consider the idea while Michael Goss argues, "There is no one theory which comfortably accounts for *all* poltergeist cases."[59]

We disagree. We are convinced that, together, the poltergeist phenomenon and its occult connection offer strong empirical evidence for the demonic nature of these spirits. In fact, we know of *no* poltergeist case that cannot be accounted for on the basis of this theory. The remainder of this section will supply evidence for our conviction. We believe the demonic theory is rejected today simply because mediums, parapsychologists and others don't like it. Thus, in spite of the evidence and the explanatory power of the demonic theory, they prefer to accept the view they personally choose to believe is true.

However, at this point we need to make two important observations. First, it is necessary to realize that poltergeist phenomena per se are *not* proof that any person supposedly psychically or otherwise associated with these events is spirit-possessed. The *person* is not causing the unusual phenomena. Again, this is an unfounded premise of the discipline of parapsychology. The poltergeist manifestations themselves are merely the result of an evil spirit working miraculous events for ulterior motives.

Second, at least temporary demonization of many individuals has occurred as a result of some poltergeist hauntings. But more often the people who experience poltergeists or are peripherally involved are simply victims, either intrigued or terrified, depending on the severity of the haunting.

We believe that an impartial evaluation of the poltergeist phenomenon itself will accomplish two things. First, it will dispel parapsychological (e.g., psychokinetic) and naturalistic (e.g., hallucinogenic) theories as not being credible. Second, it will dispel the mediumistic view by offering strong evidence that poltergeists are demons—not the confused spirits of the dead.

12. Do ghost phenomena require a supernatural explanation? And how are ghosts connected to the occult?

Considered objectively, poltergeist phenomena are very difficult to explain apart from recourse to the supernatural. Theories of natural or human origin are simply inadequate. Poltergeists involve an incredible number of diverse manifestations and unsavory incidents. These may include horrible foul smells, cold rooms, thick or oppressive air, unusual malevolent voices, bizarre, creaturely, or human apparitions, movement of objects (even very heavy ones), spontaneous fires, strange markings on furniture or people, headaches and other physical symptoms, and electromagnetic phenomena, to name a few.

In his extensive bibliography, Goss describes the following common phenomena associated with the poltergeist. Even though the poltergeist has been named after its auditory effects, other phenomena may include:

- Showers of stones, earth, mud, sticks, fruit, shells and, occasionally, more bizarre material such as banknotes, small animals, etc.;

- Objects, e.g., furniture, may be rolled, moved, overturned or otherwise agitated; in particular, small items are likely to be thrown, levitated, caused to simulate a rocking or "dancing" motion, or may be swept across the room in flights of complicated and sustained trajectory from which they descend either gradually and gently in hovering motion or very abruptly;

- Bedclothes, linen, garments and curtains may be molested, torn, slashed or otherwise damaged. In some rare cases, linen has been found to have been deliberately arranged in the form of a "tableau" reminiscent of human figures at worship;

- Small objects may disappear from their appointed places, possibly making subsequent reappearances in highly incongruous situations . . . others fail to reappear at all;
- "Apports" (objects perhaps foreign to the afflicted household) may similarly arrive on the scene;
- Manipulations suggestive of internal malfunction may affect electrical equipment later found to be in normal working order. Telephones may ring or register calls when none have been made; plugs are removed and lightbulbs smashed or wrenched from their sockets;
- "Spontaneous" fires may break out;
- Pools or jets of water (and/or liquids) may be emitted from normally dry surfaces, e.g., walls, ceilings, etc.;
- Personal assaults such as blows, slaps, shoves, etc., may be inflicted on householders and their guests. However, stigmata in the form of wheels, teeth-marks or scratches, are likely to be confined to one particular person, namely the supposed "agent" or "focus" in the disturbances;
- Apparitions (human, animal or indeterminate) are sometimes witnessed, as are unusual lights, clouds of phosphorescence, etc.;
- In a few instances a form of psychic invasion characterized as "possession" or entrancement with associated psi abilities and the poltergeist agent has been reported.[60]

As Bayless correctly reports, "with a poltergeist, every form of psychical phenomena both in the experimental seance and in spontaneous cases, has been reported, and the sheer diversity of manifestations is truly incredible. It is almost impossible to list all the strange, individual actions attributed to the poltergeist."[61]

The "Unsolved Mysteries" TV series on February 23, 1996, reported that the famous Los Angeles "Comedy Store" is subject to serious hauntings. One waitress alone had chronicled at least 50 supernatural events. Comedy stars like Arsenio Hall, Roseanne and Jim Carry first got their start here.

In the 1940s and 1950s, "The Comedy Store" was called Ciro's. It was the most popular nightclub in all Hollywood and widely considered "the place to be seen." Ciro's was frequented both by famous movie stars such as Tyrone Power, Bette Davis and Lucille Ball as well as by mob gangsters such as Mickey Coleman and Ben "Bugsy" Siegel, the murderous mobster who built The Flamingo, one of the earliest great Las Vegas casinos.

Coleman had killed a number of people, apparently at Ciro's; and, the story goes, these individuals continue today to haunt The Comedy Store. What is significant about the story is not the characteristic death connection in poltergeist events, which, as we saw supposedly confirms there is no biblical judgment at death, but the kinds of events that have happened there. Consider two examples. In one case, in a matter of just a few seconds, all the table chairs in the main-stage room were piled in a heap one on top of another. An individual was in the room and all the chairs were neatly placed around the tables; he left the room for a few seconds and came back to find them all piled in a heap. Further, not a sound was heard of the activity.

In another incident, a waitress had just finished getting the room set up for the evening's performance. She had placed tablecloths over the tables, put down ashtrays, and so forth. She left the room for a few seconds, came back, and, incredibly, found that the room was just as it was before she had fitted all the tables. In other words, in a matter of literally less than 10 seconds, all the ashtrays, tablecloths, silverware, and napkins that had been on the tables were now lying in their original positions, waiting to be placed. The tablecloths and other items were *neatly* stacked.

Obviously, things like this could hardly be the result of a mental hallucination or psychokinesis, adolescent or otherwise—especially since no adolescents were present. (In fact, have those who advocate this strained theory of adolescents and psychokinetic energy ever done a credible study to determine just how frequently adolescents are even present at poltergeist events?)

In addition, examining poltergeists as a whole, we find truly frightening apparitions that can only be characterized as demonic and which may seriously injure people. There are also horrible encounters with beings which may take grotesque human form and in rare cases proceed to kill or to sexually rape both men and women, leaving them covered with a slimy substance and/or terrible odor.[62] Further, the rare if controversial phenomenon of spontaneous human combustion—people instantaneously bursting into flames and largely being reduced to ashes—may have some kind of association with poltergeists. And, as noted, there are also numerous examples of demonic possession occurring during poltergeist manifestations.[63] Thus, in many cases investigated "the nature of the invading force has many times been annoying and malicious, and frequently has displayed a vicious and dangerous nature.... Poltergeist's intentions ... were in the main savage, destructive and malignant."[64]

It is hardly surprising then, as occult authority Colin Wilson points out, that "until the mid-nineteenth century it was generally assumed that poltergeist disturbances were the result of witchcraft, or evil spirits, or both."[65] In his bibliography, Goss points out in a similar fashion that earlier generations "concluded quite logically that they were faced by the work of witchcraft and/or demons" and that such a theory "has shown remarkable durability regardless of what the twentieth century may think about witchcraft and demons."[66]

In fact, researchers have connected the poltergeist to mediumism, witchcraft, spiritism and other forms of the occult throughout history, right up to the present. Scores of incidents were recorded or investigated by the late Dr. Kurt Koch, a leading Christian authority on the occult. In every case "occult practices lay at the root of the [poltergeist] phenomena."[67]

Indeed, what poltergeists are actually connected with is occult practices, not hallucinations or adolescent psychokinesis. This connection is illustrated by the fact that the celebrated revival of mid-nineteenth century spiritualism in America actually began with a poltergeist. The Fox sisters' "rappings" were clearly a manifestation of poltergeist activity. Colin Wilson, noted author of *The Occult: A History*, observes, "The Hydesville rappings which inaugurated the history of modern spiritualism were almost certainly poltergeist phenomena; the Hydesville 'ghost' also claimed to be the victim of an undetected murder."[68]

Once poltergeist disturbances are experienced in a home, often the Ouija board is brought out of a closet in an attempt, whether in seriousness or jest, to establish contact with the "troubled ghost." In such cases, poltergeist phenomena often become the means of a person's conversion to the occult. The supernatural encounters are so startling and intriguing that even initially skeptical observers may come to a belief in the supernatural and become involved in psychic investigation, such as seeking the advice of psychics, using automatic writing, or attending seances.

In *The Enigma of the Poltergeist*, psychical researcher Raymond Bayless further observes, "It can be suggested that witchcraft may be the child of the poltergeist. The study of poltergeists and haunting phenomena continually uncovers reminders of the close relationship existing between each subject."[69]

Poltergeist phenomena are not only frequently associated with witchcraft but with necromancy and seance phenomena as well. For example, "It [the poltergeist] has duplicated every phenomenon observed in the experimental seance."[70] And, "during known, obvious poltergeist cases, phantoms have been seen and heard that gave every indication of having been spirits of the dead. On occasion, phantoms have indicated that they were spirits of dead relatives of witnesses present."[71]

From a Christian view, we see this as a typical attempt by demons to establish belief in or practice of contacting the dead—something God has forbidden in the Bible (Deuteronomy 18:9-12). This is illustrated in the attempt to "rescue" supposedly confused or "earth-bound" spirits who are allegedly causing the poltergeist disturbances. Thus, "In each case the living had a duty to the dead. By means of seances (sometimes specifically convened as 'rescue circles') the distressed party [the poltergeist] could be contacted and ultimately directed along the appointed paths of self-improvement."[72]

In fact, we suspect that, in many cases where poltergeists *are* directly associated with some person, rather than a location, that demons are attempting to trick the individual into some kind of occult involvement or even bring about his or her possession.

At the least, when poltergeist phenomena seems to be associated with an individual, there are certain parallels to the medium and her spirit controls: "Obviously, this relates to the concept of mediumship in general and moreover to the equally fascinating study of the way in which this person—the 'agent' or 'focus'—is different from other human beings who do *not* have poltergeist abilities."[73]

In light of the above, it is not surprising that a common feature of ghost or poltergeist manifestations involves the attempt to seek actual contact with the dead. This also, obviously, is a common occurrence in seance mediumism. For example, Dr. Weldon remembers viewing a television program on a particularly dramatic poltergeist haunting in 1994. After the poltergeist manifestations began, a Ouija board was used to attempt to make contact with the spirit. Through the board, the spirit spelled out its name to those present. The next day psychical researchers were called in to investigate. Hauntingly, one of these parapsychologists had the name of this spirit mentally impressed upon him entirely without his knowledge. He simply began his conversation, "When did you first meet _____?" and gave the actual name that the spirit had given the day before through the Ouija board. He had no idea *why* he said this name or where it came from, but obviously it "confirmed" the "identity" of the spirit they were now seeking to establish contact with. Further, this particular name was, in fact, found to be that of the very same individual who had lived in that house prior to that time—and who had also been murdered. In the minds of everyone present, this confirmed the fact they were actually in contact with the deceased spirit of the man who had earlier been killed in this house. In the world of the occult, this kind of confirmatory scenario is not at all an uncommon occurrence.

13. Who do these ghosts claim to be? What are the consequences of believing in their common interpretation?

The spirits of the occult, in general, are often contacted directly by psychics, mediums or channelers. They permit themselves to become possessed by these spirits and allow those spirits to speak through them. At poltergeist hauntings, mediums or psychics may also allow themselves to be possessed in order to discover the alleged reason for the "haunting" by establishing direct contact with the "troubled ghost." Of course, in occult circles, the poltergeist is characteristically interpreted in line with prevailing beliefs about the dead, human psychokinesis, and so forth. But given the well-known ability of demons to assume virtually any shape and to take virtually any disguise, from angels to UFO aliens to the human dead, how can occultists be certain that poltergeists are what they think they are? Can mediums be certain the appearances of "dead loved ones" in seances are not the clever tricks of demons to foster emotional trust and dependence?

While speaking through human mediums, the ghosts that are contacted during poltergeist outbreaks have offered several reasons that explain their activities. First, some claim to be the spirits of the dead who were once atheists, materialists or rationalists while on earth and never expected to encounter an afterlife. Upon death, their shock was so great they became confused and disoriented. Like a lost and wounded traveler in a strange city, they wander aimlessly, attempting to get their bearings.

Second, some say they are otherwise confused spirits. Initially, some spirits of the dead supposedly refuse to believe they are really dead and are no longer able to live upon the earth. They now vainly attempt to convince themselves that they are still in their bodies and can somehow return to their previous existence. As a result, they not only seek to regain contact with the living through "haunting" houses where the living reside, but they desperately seek to manifest themselves materially in order to regain contact with the physical world. Bizarre poltergeist events are one result of their attempt to interact with and materialize back into their previous existence.

Third, some ghosts argue that they are alleged spirits of Christians who erroneously accepted the idea of a biblical heaven. Such persons are shocked, dismayed and angry to discover that the Bible they trusted was wrong. Rather than finding themselves in heaven with their Lord, they instead found themselves in the spirit world with no Jesus or heaven anywhere in sight. Some of these ghosts refuse to accept this, waiting instead for "Jesus" to come and take them to "heaven." In the meantime, they vent their confusion, anger and grief through poltergeist manifestations.

Fourth, they claim to be the spirits of the dead who were evil people involved in violent acts such as murder or rape at a particular location on earth. After death, they chose to remain close to the earth to continue their evil. Or, they are deceased victims of evil people and are frightened to go forward and progress spiritually or they wish to seek revenge on the living relatives of those who harmed them.

Finally, poltergeists may say they are the spirits of the dead who are experiencing confusion resulting from suicide. Famous medium George Anderson, who communicates regularly with alleged spirits of the dead, mentioned the following anecdote concerning his personal friend. "A friend of mine who had recently taken his life came through [me] and did not know how to go into the light. I kept telling him to go forward to the light, but he was afraid of [temporary] judgment. He couldn't forgive himself. Also, he was having a problem with the fact that after he had taken his own life, his spirit obviously lingered around the scene of the act."[74]

These are the claims of ghosts and poltergeists. But regardless of the spirits' claims, we think the demonologists of an earlier era such as de Spina (1460), Nider (1470), Remy (1595), and Guazzo (1608) were correct: These spirits are not what they claim (spirits of the human dead), but lying spirits which the Bible identifies as demons. This is strongly indicated by the fact that poltergeist claims, manifestations and results tend to have five distinct consequences—*all* of which lend greater credibility to the Christian view.

There are five consequences of accepting the common view that ghosts are the human dead or manifestations of human psychic ability.

First, as noted, poltergeist manifestations tend to involve or interest people in the occult. Poltergeist phenomena frequently cause unsuspecting people to assume the truth of an occult worldview such as mediumism, witchcraft, reincarnation and paganism. The phenomenon itself is so startling that participants become converted to belief in the supernatural and, not infrequently, end up personally involved in psychic investigation through seances, channeling, Ouija boards or various forms of divination. Thus, a parapsychologist may be called in to investigate the disturbance. Often a psychic, channeler, or medium is brought in to communicate with the troubled spirit, to attempt to "help" it or, if it is evil, to exorcise it.

Demons have a vested interest in all this because it not only supports the occult, it offers a novel and unexpected manner for them influence or contact people. Poltergeist activity encourages attempts to contact the dead—something God has forbidden as being reprehensible to Him: "Let no one be found among you who... practices divination or sorcery... engages in witchcraft... or who is a medium or spiritist or who consults the dead. Anyone who does these things is detestable to the LORD" (Deuteronomy 18:10-12).

Second, in the minds of many people, poltergeist phenomena tend to discredit the biblical view of the afterlife and of immediate judgment at death. Indeed, most people in the world do think of poltergeists as the spirits of the human dead. But if these large numbers of dead are actually roaming around the spirit world and contacting our world, then the biblical portrait of the confinement and judgment of the unregenerate at death is obviously false.

This scenario also supports the goals of demons who have a vested interest in deceiving people about biblical truth concerning the afterlife. Obviously, if there is no hell in the afterlife, there is no need for a Savior in this life. But God tells us, "Man is destined to die once, and after that to face judgment" (Hebrews 9:27). To those who reject God's gracious offer of salvation Jesus warned, "If you do not believe that I am the one I claim to be, you will indeed die in your sins" (John 8:24). The writer of Hebrews asks, "How shall we escape [judgment] if we ignore such a great salvation?" and "See to it that you do not refuse him who speaks. If they did not escape when they refused him [Moses] who warned them on earth, how much less will we, if we turn away from him [Jesus] who warns us from heaven?" (Hebrews 2:3 and 12:25). Jesus himself emphasized that the unregenerate and unrighteous "will go away to eternal punishment, but the righteous to eternal life" (Matthew 25:46).

The Bible teaches clearly that the unsaved dead are now confined in a place of punishment, while the saved dead are in glory with Christ (Luke 16:19-31; 2 Peter 2:9; Philippians 1:23; 2 Corinthians 5:6,8). Therefore, the implication most people draw from poltergeist manifestations, that the dead roam freely, is clearly false from a biblical viewpoint.

Third, poltergeist events grant spiritual authority and credibility first to the occultist (the psychic, spiritist, medium, channeler) and second to those involved with them (the parapsychologist, psychical researcher). It is these individuals who investigate the disturbance and supposedly solve the problem. Because such persons are frequently able to "resolve" the disturbance, although usually not without a battle of sorts (with the spirits gladly cooperating behind the scenes), the entire episode grants those involved in the occult, whether personally or "scientifically," a good deal of spiritual prestige. But as many former mediums have revealed, such resolutions to poltergeist hauntings are merely a ruse of the spirits to fool people into adopting unbiblical teachings or practices.* This is also something that harmonizes well with the goal of demons: to secure people's trust toward those who, however unwittingly, actively promote the demons own interests and who often actively oppose Christianity. As the history of the occult reveals, all this hinders the good purposes God has intended for man.

Fourth, concerning the parapsychological view of poltergeist phenomena being a result of human psychic potential, this confuses the realm of the psychological and the supernatural, masks the activity of demons and helps make the domain of the occult the domain of the psychologist. The popular adolescent theory suggests that when certain children approach the age of puberty, this somehow creates an excess amount of psychic energy which, in some unknown manner, is spontaneously released to create poltergeist effects. Thus, poltergeist manifestations are presumed to indicate an abnormal condition of the human mind. Therefore, the theory concludes, the true source of the poltergeist lay in the human psyche, a result of a mass

---

* For more information, read former medium Ralphael Gasson's *The Challenging Counterfeit* and Robert Curran's *The Haunted: One Family's Nightmares*.

of outwardly projected adolescent repression, fear, anger or confusion.

One consequence of the idea that poltergeist phenomena mysteriously emerge from the consciousness of adolescents is to draw child and other psychologists into the ranks of those who study poltergeist phenomena. Thus, the poltergeist becomes the natural domain of the psychologist and, from that point, the psychologist finds it easy to become entwined in the occult domain of the parapsychologist. In essence, the *psychological* theory inevitably links the poltergeist with the adolescent, the adolescent with the psychologist and the psychologist with the parapsychologist.

This consequence can be seen in the attempt to make poltergeist phenomena part of human origin which, by definition, opens the doors to exploration of human psychic potential. As no less an authority than Colin Wilson remarks, "The recognition that poltergeists are of human origin was one of the greatest intellectual landmarks in human history. It was the first convincing proof that we possess other floors"[75] (i.e., other psychic levels or dimensions within our own being).

Given the demonic nature of the poltergeist phenomena as a whole, it is rather incredible that so many otherwise rational people ascribe poltergeists to some kind of alleged spontaneous, uncontrollable, psychological/psychic (projected repressions)/ psychokinetic function of human beings. Yet parapsychologists, psychic researchers, and occultists who investigate these phenomena seem to consider the demonic theory hardly worthy of mention. But isn't the demonic theory far more believable than the idea that human psychic energy can account for the kinds of manifestations we find? Again:

> Objects are projected with alarming velocity, and often seem directly aimed at some human target. . . . Another peculiarity is the wavy path, quite irreconcilable with gravitational laws, which these projectiles often seem to follow. They turn corners, swerve in and out, and behave, in fact, like a bird which is free to pick its own way. Not less surprising is . . . that the stones and other missiles are for the most part invisible at the beginning of their flight. They do not come into view until they are just a few feet off. They enter closed rooms and seem to drop from the ceilings or to penetrate doors and windows without leaving a trace of their passage.[76]

What human being on earth, adolescent or aged, can duplicate such things? Indeed, it is the consistently supernatural nature of the phenomenon which so forcefully argues *against* a purely human origin. We believe this also advances the purpose of demons who, hiding safely behind the realms of the parapsychologist and the psychic simultaneously, promote the occult and its redefinition toward a purely psychological realm.

Fifth, poltergeists manifestations frequently harm people whether physically, emotionally or spiritually. Therefore the view of poltergeists as harmless ghosts also plays into the hands of demons. Since demons are innately evil and unredeemable, this fits well with their own desires and purposes.

In essence, all five consequences of the poltergeist are seen to support the goals of those evil spirits the Bible identifies as demons. Therefore, it is hardly out of place to suggest that poltergeists are actually a ruse of demons to further their own agendas.

14. Does Halloween support witchcraft? Is witchcraft dangerous? Are ghosts related to witchcraft?

After the idea of roaming spirits of the dead, witchcraft is perhaps the most common theme of Halloween. However, our cultural image of witchcraft is changing from that of something evil to something spiritually positive. Unfortunately, witchcraft is no laughing matter.

Leading former witch Doreen Irvine reports how the proselytizing activity of modern witches is designed to recast their tarnished image historically: "It was important to give witchcraft a new look, and these guidelines were laid down: 'never frighten anyone. Offer new realms of mystery and excitement. Make witchcraft less sinister. Make it look like a natural, innocent adventure... cover up evil with appealing wrappings...'"[77]

One way children can be deceived about witches is through their attempt to recast themselves in a benign light. Those having this agenda use Halloween to teach children that witchcraft is good and witches are genuinely spiritual people, healers, and protectors of the environment. Of course, most witches today claim to be "good" witches which causes much confusion. The truth is that in the tradition of witchcraft, so-called white witches can sometimes be just as evil as black witches. Regardless, from a biblical perspective all witchcraft is evil. Nevertheless, revisionist history continues to recast the witch and neo-pagan communities as those who would help both mankind and planet Earth itself.

In *The Anatomy of Witchcraft,* Peter Haining describes leading witch Raymond Buckland as "certainly the most important Gardnerian witch in America and perhaps the cult's most level-headed and convincing spokesman."[78] In 1994, John Weldon had a radio debate with Buckland, who, in the early 1960s, was probably the one most responsible for reintroducing modern-day witchcraft to the United States. He has written over 30 books on this subject and other aspects of the occult. In that debate, Buckland claimed the following of witchcraft: "It's just another religion...it's not antiChristian—it's nothing like that. The main message is positive.... We hold pretty much the same ideas of doing good [as Christians].... I've spoken at Roman Catholic colleges on Long Island, New York, I've spoken for Methodists, for Baptists, for Episcopalians—many, many different groups. Generally, I would say that there's been a very good reaction: 'Now this is interesting. Tell us more.' That's the sort of reaction that I've gotten rather than anything antagonistic."[79]

Buckland's view of witchcraft as something that is not antiChristian but something good and positive, is contradicted by the facts, not to mention God's own view of witchcraft. In Scripture we are told very clearly that anyone who "engages in witchcraft...is detestable to the LORD" (Deuteronomy 18:10,12).

Not too long ago *Time* magazine estimated that there were about 160,000 witches in America and possibly half as many in Britain. Obviously, painting witchcraft in a good, positive, "white" light is part of the reason for the success of witchcraft—along with the general breakdown of Western culture.

But today, even some Christians don't seem too convinced about the dangers of witchcraft. One evangelical scholar claims, "The majority of witchcraft and ritual magic appear to be relatively innocuous," even going so far as to assert that ritual magic may be "essentially harmless."[80] Again, such attitudes are contradicted by the history of witchcraft and ritual magic and the testimony of current and former practitioners, some of which we documented in *The Coming Darkness* (Harvest House Publishers, 1993). And certainly Halloween has a part to play in all this. "In the opinion of Dr. David Enoch, former senior consultant psychiatrist at the Royal Liverpool Hospital and the University of Liverpool, Halloween practices open the door to the occult and can introduce forces into people's lives that they do not understand and often cannot combat.... For too many children, this annual preoccupation...leads to a deepening fascination with the supernatural, witches and the possibility of exercising power over others."[81]

As another example, consider the following information given in *Harper's* magazine. In "Toward a more P.C. [politically correct] Halloween" we find excerpts from the teacher's manual of the *Anti-Bias Curriculum: Tools for Empowering Young Children* produced by the Anti-Bias Curriculum Task Force of Early Childhood Educators in California and published by the National Association for the Education of Young Children in Washington, D.C. In this manual we are told that the Halloween image of the witch as old, wicked, ugly and dressed in black "reflects stereotypes of gender, race, and age: 'Powerful women are evil; old women are ugly and scary; the color black is evil.'" The myth of the evil witch "reflects a history of witch-hunting and witch-burning... directed against mid-wives and other independent women." We are told that this stereotype of witches as evil should be challenged by teachers today "because it is so offensive, especially to many women."

An example is given of a teacher named Kay who did the following activities two weeks before Halloween. She first asks the children what they think about witches. She receives the standard responses of "bad, ugly, old." The teacher then says, "Many people do think that. What I know is that the real women we call witches aren't bad. They really helped people.... They healed people who were sick or hurt." This gets the children talking about doctors and the teacher replies, "Yes, the [witch] healers were like doctors."

On other days, Kay brings in various herbs showing how they were used by witches in healing and she also sets up a "witch-healer" table "where the children can make their own potions." At the end of the two-week course, children have a new consensus—that witches fall into two categories: "Some were bad, some good. So although the activities don't completely change the children's minds, they do stretch thinking by creating a category of 'some good witches.'"[82]

With tens of thousands of witches in America and an undetermined number of them teachers of young children, who would think that a time such as Halloween will not be used by them to their own advantage? Of course, witches also have a lot of help from many religious liberals, radical feminists, those in the goddess movement and among adherents of the neo-pagan revival. All of them work together to support witchcraft as a benign and spiritually divine activity—but at what cost?

What is forgotten today is that witchcraft *is* increasingly appealing to a large number of people because of the manner in which it is presented and the community and power that it offers. For example, one former witch discusses why witchcraft was so appealing to her and has become so appealing to many others: "It all seemed so harmless and so beautiful. It was a beautiful experience.... Wicca builds community. It builds community because there are so many people out there seeking this oneness with the earth, this oneness with the universe, this oneness with the ultimate god and goddess aspect. Everybody wants love, everybody wants to get along, everybody wants peace, and in Wicca, when you are involved in a group, it starts off that way."[83]

Yet Guadalupe Rosalez found another reality than the one she initially encountered. First, in contrast to the claims of Raymond Buckland cited earlier that witchcraft is not antiChristian, Rosalez found just the opposite. Having a Christian background, she wanted to use Christ in her rituals but the witchcraft council would not allow her to use the name of Christ—not even as one god among many. "They just said: 'No, you are forbidden to use Christ.'"[84] She was taken before the council several times for discussion or discipline.

(Incidentally, the modern perception that Christians were involved in the burning of witches at the Salem witch trials and elsewhere is highly distorted. For example, at the 1692 Salem trials "one of the greatest ironies of history is that Christians were accused, Christians died, Christians tried to stop the trials, and still Christianity gets the blame. Devout lay Christians... as well as devout ministers [were accused].... Marion L. Starkey proves [in *The Devil in Massachusetts: A Modern Inquiry into the Salem Witch Trials*] 'Far more ministers were making a stand against prosecution than were lending themselves to it.'... [and Chadwick Hansen in *Witchcraft at Salem* writes], 'In fact the clergy were, from beginning to end, the chief opponents to the events of Salem.'"[85] True, the majority who were executed were innocent but there were some who were genuinely guilty of witchcraft (although this did not justify their execution). In fact, Wallace Notestein observes that "good" witches would even accuse each other in order to destroy a rival witch's business.[86])

Guadalupe Rosalez also eventually found that there was a great deal of envy and animosity among her coven members. And in the end:

I saw it all for what it really was when I was trying to leave and separate myself from them. They made it hard for me. I had nightmares and visions that nobody else had and sicknesses that were not accounted for physically.... I was being pressured into going into the art of necromancy, which is raising of the dead in witchcraft.... It is just too dangerous in both a spiritual sense and a mental sense. If you are not strong enough spiritually, it will drive you crazy... I had to make a choice. It was either witchcraft or God.... To this day, almost two years later, I am still being followed. I am still being attacked on and off. I think the worst came a couple of weeks ago. I ran into this person that appeared to be demonized, on the street, and she threatened my children. She said that if I did not go back [into witchcraft] my children were going to die by the 12th of this month.... It is now after that date. I was hit pretty bad. I was sick and there was a point of stagnation where I just could not seem to move. I had no will of my own but I had much prayer through the churches and I prayed myself.... Praise God my children are now fine.[87]

She soberly tells her former witch friends that should they, too, cross the line, "You will come to the conclusion that the people you thought loved you the most, that took you into the craft, your best friends, have become your worst enemies."[88]

In *The Coming Darkness*, we spent over 300 pages documenting the dangers of occult practices. Certainly witchcraft is no harmless pastime and the use of Halloween to encourage witchcraft is terribly misguided.

The former witch cited above recalls, "[A]s a witch you always seem to seek the counsel of a spirit guide."[89] Raymond Buckland, quoted earlier, says that the focus of witchcraft is "a belief in deities, and a worship of these deities, thanking them for what we have, asking them for what we need."[90] Witchcraft, poltergeists and other forms of spiritism tend to go hand in hand. Biblically, this means that witchcraft is involved with the powers of darkness. If these spirits and ghosts are really demons, no other conclusion is possible.

Montague Summers' *Geography of Witchcraft* and *History of Witchcraft,* as well as many standard encyclopedias and compendiums on witchcraft, show the close connections between witchcraft and poltergeists. Consider the following discussion by leading occult authority Colin Wilson in his book *Poltergeist!: A Study in Destructive Haunting*. He discusses the historical connection between witchcraft, poltergeists, necromancy and spiritism and points out that writing the text of an illustrated book about witchcraft "proved to be an excellent preparation for writing a book about poltergeists."[91]

> And *all* witchcraft has been based on the idea of magic: that the witch or magician can make use of spirit entities to carry out her will. . . . the chief business of a witch in those days (about 1,000 B.C.) was *raising the dead.* And later tales of witches—in Horace, Apuleius and Lucan—make it clear that this was still true 1,000 years later on. After the beginning of the Christian era . . . the witch also became the invoker of demons. . . . In his notorious *History of Witchcraft,* the Reverend Montague Summers denounces modern Spiritualism as a revival of witchcraft. He may simply have meant to be uncomplimentary about Spiritualism; but, as it happens, he was historically correct. The kind of spiritualism initiated by the Fox sisters was the nearest approach to what Lucan's Erichtho, or Dame Alice Kyteler, would have understood by witchcraft. It begins and ends with the idea that we are surrounded by invisible spirits, including those of the dead, and that these can be used for magical purposes. . . . Witchcraft is about "spirits"—the kind of spirits we have been discussing in this book.[92]

In conclusion, Halloween, poltergeists, witchcraft and spiritism are all closely connected. This means that however innocent Halloween may be at one level, at another level its innocence is lost altogether. Further, because of the modern revival of witchcraft and other forms of neopaganism, an article on the subject in *Christianity Today* correctly reported that "profound changes are underway in the religious climate of the West. They suggest that new religious forces are nibbling at the foundations of a society and a culture built largely upon a Christian world view."[93] Indeed, they are. This is why the Christian community should be more committed to prayer, sanctification and evangelism. If we do our part, God may indeed reverse the tide.

Closing Remarks

For those people who do yet know Jesus Christ as their personal Lord and Savior, or for those who have recently come out of the occult, and desire to find the true God and eternal life (see 1 John 5:13), we would encourage them to sincerely pray the following prayer:

> Lord Jesus Christ, I *humbly acknowledge* that I have sinned in my thinking, speaking and acting, that I am guilty of deliberate wrongdoing, that my sins have separated me from Your Holy presence, and that I am helpless to commend myself to You.

I *firmly believe* that You died on the cross for my sins, bearing them in Your own body and suffering in my place the condemnation they deserved.

I *have thoughtfully counted the cost of following You*. I sincerely repent, turning away from my past sins. I am willing to surrender to You as my Lord and Master. Help me not to be ashamed of You.

So now I come to You. I believe that for a long time You have been patiently standing outside the door knocking. I now open the door. Come in, Lord Jesus, and be my Savior and my Lord forever. Amen.[94]

Becoming a Christian is a serious commitment. We encourage you to begin to read your Bible—especially the New Testament—to pray daily and to attend a church where Christ is honored and people show their love for Him by what they do.

Keeping Your Children Safe on Halloween

Young Children's Concerns

For children around the ages of three and four, Halloween can be a truly frightening time with thoughts of monsters in the closet or under the bed. Even parents donning Halloween masks in jest can be frightening and confusing to a young child. Probably the last thing a child this age will want to do is go trick-or-treating. Parents should take their child's fears seriously, even if they appear silly. They should reassure the child that they will protect him or her from any harm.

In "Why Halloween Scares Preschoolers" (*Parents* magazine, Oct. 1994), Dr. Lawrence Kutner provides a number of helpful ideas to consider, including: "If you take your child trick-or-treating, go before sunset. Darkness makes even familiar things more frightening to children." [However, his advice that "your child needs to know that ghosts are imaginary" is unsound. If your child asks about ghosts, explain at the appropriate age-level that he or she does not need to be frightened of any ghosts or spirits that might (or do) exist because Jesus will protect him or her.]

Physical Safety

1. Children should wear warm clothes under their costumes.
2. Costumes should be made of fire-retardent material.

3. The costume should be loose enough to allow freedom of movement and fit, but short enough so the child won't trip over it. (Apparently falls are the number one cause of accidents on Halloween.)

4. Decorate costumes with reflective tape or glow-in-the-dark paint.

5. Be sure that accessories, such as swords, are made with flexible materials.

6. Use safe facial make-up or make sure the mask has large openings for the nose, mouth and eyes for normal breathing and vision.

7. Give children white or luminous bags to collect their treats in.

8. Provide a small flashlight for your trick-or-treater.

9. Work out the trick-or-treating route in advance, establish a return time and provide change for a phone call in case the child becomes lost or needs help.

10. Emphasize safety rules regarding traffic, strangers, etc.

11. As a general guideline, children under 12 should be accompanied by an adult; children over 12 should trick-or-treat in groups.

12. Stress that your child should bring candy home for inspection before eating. Eating a substantial dinner before trick-or-treating may help.

13. Sort through the candy, and throw away any questionable items.[95]

NOTES

Section I

1. Jennifer deCoursey, "Monster Event for Marketers," *Advertising Age*, Oct. 16, 1995, pp. 1, 40.

2. Ruth Hutchison and Ruth Adams, *Every Day's a Holiday* (New York: Harper & Brothers, 1951), p. 235.

3. Q.v., "Celtic Religion," *Encyclopedia Britannica*, Macropedia, vol. 3.

4. Julius Caesar, *Commentaries,* Book 6, Chapter 18.

5. Becky Stevens Cordello, *Celebrations* (Butterick Publishing, 1977), p. 112.

6. Robert J. Myers, *Celebrations: The Complete Book of American Holidays* (Garden City, New York: Doubleday & Co., 1972), p. 259.

7. Ethel L. Urlin, *Festivals, Holy Days and Saint's Days: A Study in Origins and Survivals in Church Ceremonies and Secular Customs* (London: Simpkin, Marshall, Hamilton, Kent & Co., 1915, republished Detroit: Gale Research Co., 1979), p. 190.

Section II

8. Q.v. "Halloween," *Encyclopedia Britannica*, Macropedia, vol. 4.

9. See Cordello, p. 114.

10. Myers, p. 260.

11. Carol Barkin and Elizabeth James, *The Holiday Handbook* (New York: Clarion, 1994), p. 41.

12. Myers, p. 261.

Section III

13. Father Andy Costello, "Sin Is a Boomerang," *U.S. Catholic*, Nov. 1992, pp. 37-38; George William Douglas, *The American Book of Days* (New York: H.W. Wilson, 1938), p. 548.

14. Despite Catholic claims, the best defense of purgatory is found in only a few verses in a noninspired text, 2 Maccabees 12:41-45, which 1) does not mention purgatory and 2) rejects Catholic doctrine by teaching the deliverance of soldiers who had died in the mortal (hence unforgivable) sin of idolatry. Alleged biblical Scriptures in support require an extremely forced exegesis. In his *Systematic Theology* (1974, p. 687), Louis Berkhof writes, "The doctrine finds absolutely no support in Scripture, and moreover, rests on several false premises" including the insufficiency of Christ's atonement; that our good works are meritorious before God and that the Church can shorten or terminate purgatorial sufferings. Cf., John Ankerberg, John Weldon, *Catholics and Protestants* (Chattanooga, TN: Ankerberg Theological Research Institute, 1994), pp. 192-94.

15. F.X. Shouppe, *Purgatory: Explained by the Lives and Legends of the Saints* (Rockford, IL: Tan Books, 1973).

16. Urlin, p. 201.

17. Costello, p. 39.

18. Ibid.

19. Ibid., p. 37.

20. Myers, p. 258.

21. Urlin, p. 195.

22. Ibid., p. 198.

23. Dorothy Gladys Spicer, *Festivals of Western Europe* (New York: H.W. Wilson, 1958), p. 17.

24. Urlin, p. 202.

25. Margaret Read MacDonald, ed., *The Folklore of World Holidays* (Detroit: Gale Research, Inc., 1992), p. 521.

26. Spicer, p. 47.

27. Hutchison and Adams, p. 236.

28. Gail S. Cleere, "Halfway to Winter," *Natural History*, Oct. 1992, p. 74.

29. George William Douglas, *The American Book of Days* (New York: H.W. Wilson, 1983), pp. 544, 545.

30. Cordello, p. 119.

31. Joseph Gaer, *Holidays Around the World* (Boston: Little Brown & Co., 1955), pp. 155-56.

32. MacDonald, p. 520.

33. Hutchison and Adams, p. 236.

34. Douglas, p. 542.

35. Ibid.

36. Myers, p. 262.

37. Ibid., p. 259.

38. Douglas, p. 543.

39. Ibid.

40. MacDonald, p. 520.

41. Douglas, p. 539.

42. Sue Ellen Thompson and Barbara W. Carlson, comp., *Holidays, Festivals, and Celebrations of the World Dictionary* (Detroit, MI: Omnigraphics, Inc., 1994), p. 132.

43. DeCoursey, p. 41.

44. Margot Adler, *Drawing Down the Moon: Witches, Druids, Goddess-worshipers, and other Pagans in America Today* (New York: The Viking Press, 1979), p. 108.

45. Costello, p. 38.

46. The divergent emphasis on nature and Satan, respectively, differences in ritual, etc., cannot obscure the commonalities in source of power, psychic development, antiChristian worldview, use of spirits, use of evil, and so on.

47. Any serious study of biblical demonology will reveal Satan as the power behind false religion, witchcraft, idolatry and the occult.

48. Doreen Irvine, *Freed from Witchcraft* (Nashville: Thomas Nelson, 1973), pp. 94-95.

49. Lewis Spence, *The History and Origins of Druidism* (London: Aquarian Press, 1971), p. 104ff.

50. Q.v. "Celtic Religion," *Encyclopedia Britannica Macropaedia*, vol. 3, p. 1069.

51. Spence, p. 159; cf. *Encyclopedia Britannica Macropaedia*, p. 1071.

52. NIV textnote on 1 Corinthians 10:18.

53. Spence, pp. 104-09.

54. Urlin, p. 202.

55. D. Scott Rogo, *The Poltergeist Experience* (New York: Penguin Books, 1979), p. 40.

56. Michael Goss, comp., *Poltergeists: An Annotated Bibliography of Works in English, Circa 1880–1970* (Metuchen, NJ: Scarecrow, 1979), p. vii.

57. Robert Curran, *The Haunted: One Family's Nightmare* (New York: St. Martins Press, 1988), p. 101.

58. Rogo, p. 284.

59. Goss, p. xi.

60. Ibid., pp. iii–iv.

61. Raymond Bayless, *The Enigma of the Poltergeist* (West Nyack, New York: Parker, 1967), p. 2.

62. See Rogo, p. 284, and Curran, pp. 114-17, 226-27.

63. See, for example, Bayless., pp. 158-74.

64. Ibid., p. 159.

65. Colin Wilson, *Mysteries: An Investigation into the Occult, the Paranormal and the Supernatural* (New York: G. P. Putnam's Sons, 1978), p. 461.

66. Goss, p. viii.

67. Wilson, pp. 462-63.

68. Kurt Koch, *Christian Counseling and Occultism* (Grand Rapids: Kregel Publishers, 1982), p. 181.

69. Bayless, p. 158.

70. Ibid., p. 9.

71. Ibid., p. 205.

72. Goss, p. ix.

73. Ibid., p. xii.

74. Joel Martin and Patricia Romanowski, *We Don't Die: George Anderson's Conversations with the Other Side* (New York: Berkeley Books, 1989), p. 242.

75. Wilson, p. 493.

76. Herbert Thurston, *Ghosts and Poltergeists* (Chicago: Henry Regnery, 1954), pp. 346-47.

77. Irvine, pp. 101-02.

78. Peter Haining, *The Anatomy of Witchcraft* (New York: Taplinger, 1972), p. 93.

79. "Getting Serious About Witchcraft in America," interview with John Weldon and Raymond Buckland, *Rutherford* magazine, Aug. 1994, pp. 16-18.

80. I. Hexham, q.v. "Satanism and Witchcraft" in Walter A. Elwell ed., *Evangelical Dictionary of Theology* (Grand Rapids: Baker Book House, 1984), p. 974.

81. Russ Parker, *Battling the Occult* (Downer's Grove, IL: InterVarsity Press, 1990), p. 35.

82. "Toward a More P.C. Halloween," excerpts from the *Anti-Bias Curriculum: Tools for Empowering Young Children* by Louise Derman-Sparks and the Anti-Bias Curriculum Task Force as given in *Harper's Magazine*, October 1991, pp. 19, 21.

83. Aida Besancon Spencer, et al., *The Goddess Revival* (Grand Rapids: Baker Book House, 1995), pp. 198-99.

84. Ibid., p. 200.

85. Ibid., pp. 276-77.

86. *A History of Witchcraft in England from 1558 to 1718*, pp. 22-23, in Ibid., p. 278.

87. Ibid., pp. 200-01.

88. Ibid., p. 203.

89. Ibid.

90. "Getting Serious" interview, p. 17.

91. Colin Wilson, *Poltergeist!: A Study in Destructive Haunting* (New York: Wideview/Perigee, 1981), p. 319.

92. Ibid., pp. 320-21.

93. Dave Bass, "Drawing Down the Moon," *Christianity Today*, April 29, 1991, p. 14.

94. Taken from John Stott, *Becoming a Christian* (Downer's Grove, IL: InterVarsity Press, 1950), p. 25.

95. These suggestions were culled from various sources, in particular, *Parents* magazine, October 1994.